Y0-BLW-899

Presented to

_____

On this _____ *day*

of _____

By _____

With this special message:

_____

_____

_____

ittybittybooks

MY PLACE IN THE SUN

THOMAS NELSON PUBLISHERS
Nashville, Tennessee

Copyright © 1994 by Thomas Nelson Publishers.

Published in Nashville, Tennessee by Thomas Nelson Publishers.

All Scripture quotations are from the NEW KING JAMES VERSION of the Bible. Copyright © 1979, 1980, 1982 by Thomas Nelson Publishers.

Library of Congress Cataloging-in-Publication Data

My place in the sun.
    p. cm. — (Itty Bitty books)
    ISBN 0-8407-6325-5
  1. Quotations, English. I. Series: Itty Bitty book.
PN6081.M9   1994
082—dc20   93-24365
                                         CIP

Printed in Singapore.
1 2 3 4 5 6 7 8 9 — 97 96 95 94

INTRODUCTION

Here's to you! You deserve accolades for your hard work and accomplishments. The words within are in honor of your perseverance and indomitable spirit and most of all your success. This tribute is given with love and admiration for YOU. God made you special and unique and He must be as proud of you as I am. God bless you!

The Lord bless and keep you; The Lord make His face shine upon you, And be gracious to you; The Lord lift up His countenance upon you, And give you peace.

NUMBERS 6:24-26

And your life would be brighter than noonday. Though you were dark, you would be like the morning. And you would be secure, because there is hope.

JOB 11:17-18

The size of your mountain is determined by your perception of it. If you think it's unconquerable, then it is. If you think you can overcome it, then you can.

UNKNOWN

If you do not think about the future, you cannot have one.

JOHN GALSWORTHY

Cause me to hear Your lovingkindness in the morning, For in You do I trust; Cause me to know the way in which I should walk, For I lift up my soul to You.

PSALM 143:8

A good laugh is sunshine in a house.

WILLIAM MAKEPEACE THACKERAY

If you have built castles in the air, that is where they should be. Now put foundations under them.

HENRY DAVID THOREAU

Life is not a having and a getting, but a being and a becoming.

MATTHEW ARNOLD

The kingdom of God is within you.

Luke 17:21

Challenges make you discover things about yourself that you never really knew.

CICELY TYSON

The future is not something we enter. It is something we create.

LEONARD I. SWEET

Life is either a daring adventure or nothing.

HELEN KELLER

Our greatest glory consists not in never falling, but in rising every time we fall.

OLIVER GOLDSMITH

We lose vigor through thinking continually the same set of thoughts. New thought is new life.

PRENTICE MULFORD

You must scale the mountain if you would view the plain.

CHINESE PROVERB

The United States Constitution doesn't guarantee happiness, only the pursuit of it. You have to catch up with it yourself.

BENJAMIN FRANKLIN

After every storm the sun will smile; for every problem there is a solution, and the soul's indefeasible duty is to be of good cheer.

WILLIAM R. ALGER

Life is worth living . . . since it is what we make it.

MATTHEW ARNOLD

We can do no great things—only small things with great love.

MOTHER TERESA

Success is relevant to coping with obstacles. . . . But no problem is ever solved by those, who, when they fail, look for someone to blame instead of something to do.

FRED WAGGONER

To believe in heaven
is not to run away from life;
it is to run toward it.

JOSEPH D. BLINCO

May the God of hope fill you with all joy and peace in believing, that you may abound in hope.

Romans 15:13

Kites rise highest against the wind, not with it.

WINSTON CHURCHILL

"For I will restore health to you and heal you of your wounds," says the Lord.

JEREMIAH 30:17

Sorrows are like thunderclouds—in the distance they look black; over our heads, scarcely gray.

JEAN PAUL RICHTER

The best way to have a good idea is to have lots of ideas.

LINUS PAULING

Man is happy only as he finds a work worth doing—and does it well.

E. MERRILL ROOT

This above all: to thine own self be true. And it must follow as the night the day, Thou canst not then be false to any man.

WILLIAM SHAKESPEARE

Your perception of life is mostly a reflection of what you look like on the inside.

J. DONALD FREESE

The way I see it, if you want the rainbow, you gotta put up with the rain.

DOLLY PARTON

I find the great thing in this world is not so much where we stand as in what direction we are moving.

OLIVER WENDELL HOLMES

Write it on your heart that every day is the best day in the year.

RALPH WALDO EMERSON

Go forth into the busy world and love it. Interest yourself in its life, mingle kindly with its joys and sorrows.

RALPH WALDO EMERSON

Success is never final; failure is never fatal; it is courage that counts.

WINSTON CHURCHILL

When spring is dancing among the hills, one should not stay in a little dark corner.

KAHLIL GIBRAN

God has put something noble and good into every heart His hand created.

MARK TWAIN

God is our refuge and strength, a very present help in trouble.

Psalm 46:1

"Hope" is the thing with feathers
That perches in the soul,
And sings the tune without the words,
And never stops at all.

EMILY DICKINSON

Comedy is medicine.

TREVOR GRIFFITHS

Happiness is a habit—cultivate it.

ELBERT HUBBARD

It is neither wealth nor splendor but tranquility and occupation which give happiness.

THOMAS JEFFERSON

Giving up is the ultimate tragedy.

ROBERT DONOVAN

Hope is not a dream, but a way of making dreams become reality.

L. J. SUENENS

It is hard to fail, but it is worse never to have tried to succeed.

THEODORE ROOSEVELT

There is no medicine like hope, no incentive so great, and no tonic so powerful as expectation of something tomorrow.

O. S. MARDEN

Happiness is found along the way—not at the end of the road.

SOL GORDON

Self-trust is the first secret of success.

RALPH WALDO EMERSON

What you think of yourself is much more important than what others think of you.

SENECA

Love comforteth like sunshine after rain.

WILLIAM SHAKESPEARE

If life were predictable, it would cease to be life and would be without flavor.

ELEANOR ROOSEVELT

Just as there comes a warm sunbeam into every cottage window, so comes a love-beam of God's care and pity for every separate need.

NATHANIEL HAWTHORNE

He who binds to himself a joy
Does the winged life destroy;
But he who kisses the joy as it flies
Lives in eternity's sunrise.

WILLIAM BLAKE

Nothing can bring you peace but yourself.

RALPH WALDO EMERSON

The hopeful man sees success where others see failure, sunshine where others see shadows and storm.

O. S. MARDEN

Now faith is the substance of things hoped for, the evidence of things not seen.

HEBREWS 11:1

I am not concerned that you have fallen; I am concerned that you arise.

ABRAHAM LINCOLN

Hard work keeps the wrinkles out of the mind and spirit.

HELENA RUBINSTEIN

You can't do anything about the length of your life, but you can do something about its width and depth.

EVAN ESAR

We make a living by what we get, but we make a life by what we give.

WINSTON CHURCHILL

Blessed are the happiness makers. Blessed are they who know how to shine on one's gloom with their cheer.

HENRY WARD BEECHER

Life gives to every man a staff and a scale of notes. The song he sings is one of his own fashioning.

ALMA LONSDALE

Those who live on the mountain have a longer day than those who live in the valley. Sometimes all we need to brighten our day is to rise a little higher.

S. J. BARROWS

Hope deferred makes the heart sick, But when the desire comes, it is a tree of life.

Proverbs 13:12

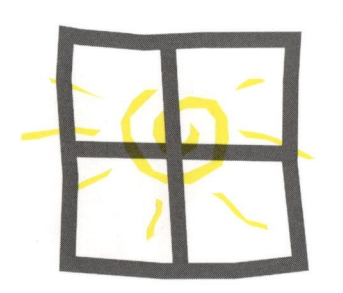

The value of life lies not in the length of days, but in the use we make of them.

MICHEL DE MONTAIGNE

He who is firm in will molds the world to himself.

GOETHE

I am a great believ in luck, and I find the harder I work the more I have of it.

STEPHEN LEACOC

Blessed is he who has learned to laugh at himself, for he shall never cease to be entertained.

JOHN BOWELL

Courage—an independent spark from heaven's bright throne, by which the soul stands raised triumphant, high, alone.

GEORGE FARQUHAR

To climb steep hills
requires slow pace at first.
WILLIAM SHAKESPEARE

Life is something like a trumpet. If you don't put anything in it, you don't get anything out. And that's the truth.

W. C. Handy

Daylight will peep through a very small hole.

JAPANESE PROVERB

There is no education like adversity.

BENJAMIN DISRAELI

A man is not what he thinks he is, but what he thinks, he is.

MAX R. HICKERSON

Dost thou love life? Then do not squander time, for that's the stuff life is made of.

BENJAMIN FRANKLIN

Seek not greatness, but seek truth and you will find both.

HORACE MANN

No one can make you feel inferior without your consent.

ELEANOR ROOSEVELT

You must have long-range goals to keep you from being frustrated by short-range failures.

CHARLES C. NOBLE

Our dignity is not in what we do but what we understand. The whole world is doing things.

GEORGE SANTAYANA

Time ripens all things. No man's born wise.

CERVANTES

Because you have occasional low spells of despondency, don't despair. The sun has a sinking spell every night but it rises again all right the next morning.

HENRY VAN DYKE

Vision is the art of seeing things invisible.

JONATHAN SWIFT

Vision is the art of seeing things invisible.

JONATHAN SWIFT

If you think you can win, you can win. Faith is necessary to victory.

WILLIAM HAZLITT

Lose as if you like it; win as if you were used to it.

TOMMY HITCHCOCK

Wonder is the beginning of wisdom.

GREEK PROVERB

Far and away, the best prize that life offers is the chance to work hard at work worth doing.

THEODORE ROOSEVELT

To travel hopefully is a better thing than to arrive.

ROBERT LOUIS STEVENSON

Write Thy blessed name, O Lord, upon my heart, there to remain so engraven that no prosperity, no adversity, shall ever move me from Thy love.

THOMAS A KEMPIS

Peace I leave with you, My peace I give to you. . . . Let not your heart be troubled, neither let it be afraid.

JOHN 14:27